I0541493

Understanding Madness

with collages by the author

Carlo Levy

2018

Seattle

ATOPON BOOKS

Atopon Books
907 15th Street
Santa Monica, California 90403
United States

Publisher's Cataloging-in-Publication data

Name: Levy, Carlo, author.
Title: Understanding madness / Carlo Levy.
Description: Santa Monica, CA: Atopon Books, 2023.
Identifiers: LCCN 2022946948 | ISBN: 979-8-9862104-2-1
Subjects: LCSH Poets--Washington (State)--Seattle
--Biography. | Creative nonfiction | Literature and mental illness. | BISAC POETRY / American / General |
BIOGRAPHY AND AUTOBIOGRAPHY / Personal
Memoirs
Classification: LCC PS3619.A8439 U58 2023 | DDC
813.6--dc23

Printed in the United States of America.

*With gratitude for the inspi-
ration and opportunity of
the Writing Groups I have
attended over the years at
the Community Psychiatric
Clinic, Wallingford*

The Bookstore
and the Voice of Reason

Several years ago I traded in a used book titled *Understanding Madness*, a book not often seen, with a swirling green and silver cover of wavy lines. Collecting experiments of people's sensory habits, how some hear extra sounds, or blame more often mysterious agents outside themselves, even believing Influencing Machines are nearby with them in mind, the compassionate author and psychologist working in contemporary London had gathered proofs, authentic examples of illusions, to illuminate the riddle of madness. Stubbornly I was too proud to keep such a solution in my small library at home. I let my faulty memory create another book, a bit murky, with images or emotions and notions developing in my mind, like musical notes, or dry seeds to feed the birds in winter, stored in a jar on a shelf, near rubber bands and wooden clothespins, or pencils for drawing clouds in the sky.

Sometimes words fade into silence, shadows, and random, lost signals I am unable to bring back to life, even if I want to keep a book forever. My mom's beautiful voice and smile have lasted all these years. I know she recognizes some quality in me that is still the same, but where have I gone? When we lived in Volunteer Park, near my grammar school, she called me from the porch, above the slope of the yard, calling me home, singing "Carlovski!" I heard her from far away, where I played in the neighborhood, becoming a character in her Thrift Store opera, happily, with echoes of her tailored clothes from a small town near Mt. Rainier, and her old school, Peabody Conservatory of Music. The trolley bus still circles down the narrow side street behind our old house and past the cemetery, back to the park I explored on foot to climb the trees and stone camels.

After reading the author's book, I appreciated his concerns, and I knew he wasn't being only scientific, or suggesting an ending to my imaginative education, and I do want to be healthy.

His book almost satisfied my character as a reader and as an example of a troubled man, but I felt something was missing, if only a place to rest and dream, some idea of the ethereal influences between beings of all kinds. After I traded it in I saw the book displayed in the window of the shop in the sunlight a few weeks later, but then it disappeared, purchased by another curious soul. I walk by the bookstore each time I am in the neighborhood, turning the corner, remembering when I lived in a studio apartment one floor above in the old building with the carved wooden door. Thirty years ago I had no telephone in my apartment and made calls from a phone booth on the sidewalk by the store. Now I look in the windows for an interesting book, and often go inside to browse, playing another small role, as a reader, wondering a little about my reception, not quite a stranger.

We are characters continuing each other's books, trying to comprehend the words around us, becoming captivated or disenchanted, or forgetful. Whose perspective becomes sensible? A bookstore has a time machine around every shelf, the outlook of countless worlds.

Being in some way responsible for the fate of others brings feelings of vertigo, a view, trying to follow the consequences, like following the spidery lines dreamed up by a hermetic philosopher hundreds of years ago, when the sky was young, leading to a diagram of the earth and heaven. So then I want to hide, become quiet and seek my own answers, in a kind of solitude, hoping to find in a neglected book a delightful friend reminding me again of loved ones.

Growing old shows me the odd serendipity between books, between people, instead of time lost in schemes conspiring against me, yet I can't forget my mistakes and bad manners. My conscience is filled with events from long ago, and yesterday, good and bad, like winning a race in school, or harming someone, acquiring a pair of glasses, losing someone, or finding a basketball card. A photograph of a beautiful face can tentatively begin an account, years later, of something unrelated, and then this fiction creates a secret world of ghosts and voices, who describe a story inside my mind that becomes more real than what I was born knowing. An abandoned manuscript weighs me down, as I carry it on my back, and now I am burdening you with it.

Everyone knows Magus Books, in the University District: "Scholarly and General Used Books, Since 1978," one block from campus. When I lived above the bookstore I started writing poetry, attending a class taught by Nelson Bentley, the beloved poet and teacher, a visionary, who wrote long apocalyptic poems, in an odd, original style, a prophet who liked the Marx Brothers, the funny pages, and nonsense verse of Edward Lear. If you met him you wouldn't consider him mad. He was wise, humorous, with a kind, honest smile and the informal grace of a rare eccentric. In his poems he called out against corruption and greed, after eating leaves of the Bible for nourishment, against the tyranny of the day, Nixon, and Reagan, against pollution and war. The spirits of Blake, Whitman, Harpo Marx, Theodore Roethke, and W.C. Fields appeared before him, choosing Nelson to speak out, in charming, vivid pictures, as the ghost of Uncle Wiggily, his 1950 Chevrolet, carried them all along through time, through the natural landscapes of the colorful narrative poems.

Often people join poetry and madness together in a circle of mutual influence. When I started writing poetry and going to the Extravaganzas and other evening readings Nelson organized I began to neglect my other studies, and I fell in love with a woman who had grown up writing in the community. That time of happiness ended sadly and ever since, my role in the world of local industry has been open to question, a bothersome customer of the Blue Museum of Seclusion.

Luckily, I met a painter who had returned home to Seattle, bringing with her a small, wooden triptych. The Sun Hearth Pyramid lit one panel from below with color, night sky and foliage, three stories, opening on twin hinges of Brooklyn and Jerusalem. Now our creations of three decades, on the Tea House schedule, poems and articles, particles, collages, dusty, magical alphabets, acorns and oils, linoleum blocks, fill closets, computer files and boxes, publications, shelves and dressers, without children to notice or care about our fate.

(She wouldn't want me to talk too much about her, so I will try to keep quiet.)

My wife is careworn from listening, and thoughtful, like you, my reader, quite spirited and decisive, about what is real and imaginary. We describe our dreams during the day's routine, shoes, dishes, keys, pillows and windows. Meanwhile my file at the Community Psychiatric Clinic grows longer. The patient counselors hope my monologues will lead Somewhere so I can learn Something about life, instead of dissolving into the aether. Maybe I could find my librarian's signal, and tune into a station where the melancholy angel of Aby Warburg teaches and Frances Yates reads from her Art of Memory. The art of conversation is difficult for me to learn, so I miss many methods of understanding madness. I should listen now and acknowledge your influence.

When I was part of a writing group at the clinic, I was asked to describe a wish, something I would hope someday to find myself doing, and I immediately thought of being in a bookstore, organizing the shelves or opening boxes. People could visit and have a cup of tea. I would have regular hours and sell items I had collected without worrying about money. The artwork on the walls would be from friends. I could offer journals from the past, like *Kayak*, *Io*, *Tree*, *Locus Solus*, *Caliban*, *Fine Madness*, and *City Lights*. The windows would let in the sunlight and the shop would be warm in the winter, and in the rain, heated by old radiators. Perhaps the windows would become foggy but there would be no mildew and only a little dust. When people came in from the cold through the door some might have to take off their glasses to wipe the steam off the lenses, then their eyes would adjust as they looked around the room, smiling and squinting a little to focus on all the objects and colors in this utopia.

I would sell my favorite books, always able to keep an edition on hand. People would become regular visitors, telling stories of the day, not always buying anything at all, just stopping by to visit. I would learn about many aspects of the city's people, the lives of artists and writers and of course readers. Over the years the shop would become known to some, but would be hidden also, a little lost in the city, from another time.

What would I learn about madness if I had these conversations, out in the world, offering books in my bookstore? There are bookstores almost like this already in Seattle, places I visit often, so what am I waiting for, a miracle? Life is bewildering and we don't always want to face up to the truth about ourselves. One bookstore I visit, in Wallingford, Open Books: A Poem Emporium, is so important in my education I should write a song cycle of thankfulness, but I can't carry a tune and I'm tone deaf, running out of ink and memory.

What has happened to the Book of the World? The bees are dying, and the glaciers are disappearing. What kind of food will we eat? The oceans are losing oxygen. Floods and droughts bring the world great suffering. Nelson would still be writing his apocalyptic poems, locating again the tyrants, like Trump, but his thoughts would be joyful, as he told us, in the Grayland Apocalypse, "...despite the national crisis. In a happy trance, I was somewhat surprised to see twelve angels wandering toward me along the tideline."

My grandmother lived in Grayland by the ocean when she was older. I remember how the road divided her house from the sand dunes where I played. I imagine I heard the waves but the ocean was far away for me. The dunes seemed so quiet, low hills of sand laced together with minerals and plants. What was the sky resolving above my tiny, preoccupied shape?

The Curse

I'm talking with myself again, trapped in a paradox with you, my reader, as if you were a spirit. Something reveals the small conspiracies in words unresolved, eggs unbroken before the Feast of Conversation. Are the voices I hear messages from the impossible city whose thoughts become the electricity of images? Should I believe in magic at all, in any of the names of faith? Your answers wouldn't be simple.

Once I knew a poet who was so angry with me she cursed me with all her heart. In her poems magical situations appear, whimsically in tune. Did her curse change my picture of time? I want to believe it became a cocoon around the past for something else to form, perhaps the hope I could become reasonable. Thirty years have passed so I can hear the voices in her poems more clearly than the sound of her cursing me.

After we decided to live apart, after my heart was broken, I told her younger sister a secret: I thought she was beautiful and I had always been attracted to her. Can you believe I was so mean and stupid? I always knew the older sister was also beautiful, and I loved her more. I had stumbled into the land of terrible disappointment and carelessness. The older sister uncovered the secret from a friend in our small world, and the curse appeared like a storm, her face shuddering, focusing behind a mysterious camera seeing many different lives in the future, all at once. Like starting to write a poem, without knowing the ending, she may have opened a crack in the sidewalk, putting a grain of rice there for a pigeon, for me, but the door in the stone closed. I became a goat nodding my head, then a child holding a piece of melting ice, and what harm could that do? A child is filled with a dark, false innocence, only alive in a book.

What were the books I read when I was young, the fantastic, weird lands of adolescence where I travelled? When I read them again details, tempers and themes reappear and I understand how time worked the stories into dreams. What I forgot haunts me. Words reach my sanctuary, simultaneously jumbled in the little forest on the map of an imaginary world, puzzling my sense of distance. Strange characters look out, floating through the Author, their voices sounding inside me like overheard, accidental logic becoming familiar, just other people like me.

They live Somewhere and answer for themselves, inside my wavering borders, where Someone hears my thoughts. Somehow there are characters who learn how to speak only the truth, who can see through my mistakes. There are ways to tell if my character is without empathy. Emotions of discovery appear in the character's vision but someone was already there, waiting. My delusions are described in old words returning from the past. I drink in the sour potion of voices, an audience who contradicts me.

I have hurt others with my bitter words and actions. Sometimes I have felt a sullen mixture of love and fear of women, like the feelings of a terrible Saint who only has a crow for a friend, after swallowing a strange drug in the medieval woods near his hermitage. Words of a sick crow, clumsy wings, knee of a walrus, my reputation in dreams and the city couldn't stop my feet, the hands of the clock, the sun, climbing up and down the steep stairs, crossing back and forth, following me to work.

I didn't know that slowly I would lose my sense of reality and be diagnosed with a mysterious disease, schizophrenia. What would happen to my eyes? I am still too young to understand. My left eye changes more often than my right, opening and closing as spirits go through the bridge between us, between one side of me and the other. My eyes become still, like dark, or pale, written words needing your sympathy, the sympathy of readers, but I'm glad you have ideas of your own.

Not too long ago the older sister called me on the telephone. She wanted to apologize for any harm she may have caused me, and I answered I was the one who should apologize for harming her. I would tell you more of the story, but I should respect her privacy. Have I said too much already? Who are my readers, and how can I address an audience without having plans for the future, except to apologize, and hope I won't trouble you anymore?

The history of madness shows the whole subject is uncertain, haphazard and hard to pin down, constantly evolving, like my own attempts to explain my story. Will you think I am blaming others for my malady? That is not my intention at all. No one who appears in these pages is to blame and I want to write about love as much as madness. Yet making my own special entry in the encyclopedia of the city is a sign of madness I am ashamed of sharing, my mistaken sense of self-importance, as if history didn't show the ordinary patterns of my life. How can I still hope you will view me as a humble person making a worthwhile effort if my perspective is so limited?

Witch in a Book

We often dream at night of curious, illustrated books we can look at closely, so strangely constructed they could only exist in the dreams, but I may be mistaken. The books don't remind us of books we have seen in museums. They seem from a time separate from any chronological expectation. They aren't necessarily modern either, and we never dream of the same book twice. They don't seem to be ours, though they arrive in our minds.

Who is showing us the book in the dream, purposefully, a book they have made for that place in the dream? Somehow they know how to do this. Yesterday one of my friends told me she was sure others looked at our own dream books, even if we were unaware of making them ourselves.

"I don't think we should argue," I said. "The important thing is how we feel when we see the illustrations in our dreams, the wonderful surprise."

"I don't want to worry about whose they are, who made them, or who is seeing them over our shoulders."

I always wonder if she knows more than I do because whenever I learn about myself and how people might be behaving, I sense they already learned this lesson before me but knew I'd have to understand on my own. That's what I mean by wanting to trust my friends. I have moments of doubt and even resentment, and then I have to reassure myself. We could easily believe many things.

Today I sat in the backyard in the sunshine for the first time in a long while, protected from the wind. Maybe in a few weeks I'll be outside more often. Then I came in and opened the front door as the sun came around. I heard some voices, actual voices and laughter. Some girls were jumping onto the hedge. I had to go outside and tell them, "Please, don't jump on the hedge."

Children often have nothing better to do than jump on a hedge. I imagined somehow they know about me, here inside, that they were risking falling into my mind, because they'd heard rumors. They were reassuring each other there was nothing to worry about.

Father of Cats

My father writes letters from Mexico describing his many cats, how they comfort him, how they are becoming old, their ailments, and I write back with news of our dog, Emma, the walks we take, her domestic habits, and also her illnesses as she gets older, as the years go by, and this is how I feel reassured my father cares for me and how I remind him I have concern for his life.

I think of him living with his second wife and all their cats, I forget how many, six or seven, or less now that Sola and Fluff have died, and I imagine this family in Mexico, and his reading quietly, cats sleeping on his lap or on a book, on a table, cats sunning themselves on the rooftop garden and I see in his letters and photographs how my father who once was selfish became a father to cats, after leaving his old family behind.

So there is another place, a land of letters, letters without arguments, faithful letters instead of betrayal, that old history of betrayal that took so long to change into stories about animals, the only children in this new land. I will never visit my father again and he is too old to travel north, but he has become so kind in this new land that sometimes I wonder what it would be like to sit and talk with him, but then I remember the way the Letter World was built, inch by inch, page by page, opening the envelopes at great distances from each other, and how we imagined each other, and I think of my mom and how she healed herself until she acquired a strange, almost alarming sense of humor and joy with no need for him anymore, and I feel our distance sustains us.

I go back to thoughts of his cats, of our dog, the characters we talk of in the faithful world, and animals become almost like people, with stubborn personalities, and we become almost like animals, essentially mysterious: chimerical, hiding in daydreams.

Emma sometimes reminds me of a deer, with soft ears and brown eyes, and sometimes a coyote, wild and aloof, or a puppy, playful and curious.

My father's cats are more complicated to him, and Emma is more involved to me, than the pictures we form in our imaginations, because we live with them ourselves, of course, but my ideas of archetypes of cats, the spirits of animals, have slowly changed, travelling toward me from Mexico, and returning from my childhood in Santa Monica, where our cat, Peep, wandered into our yard one day, in the past, as Emma travels to the future where I grow older, as my imagination alters in odd ways, knowing these imaginary animals, alongside the perishable, aging companions. I'm less lonely now in this Land of Animals where my father's concern for me grows in each letter, as if after he dies we will keep hearing from each other in the images and words of the city, and after Emma dies, there won't be any time without her, in the Land of Letters or here where we feed her.

The Great Project

For many years I thought my father might be working on a strange project, something close to him, something that would reveal the elements of his world. Ever since I could remember he sat by himself on the sofa with a small notebook on his knee, often closing his eyes in thought, then making a few notes, something old, I imagined, a mystery of names, not my heroes, Maury Wills, or Happy Hairston, or Bilbo, but echoes of William Wordsworth, Hazlitt, and revolutions, and Plato, his friends who considered his soul whereas I was only a bad actor, he told me, when I tried to be funny at dinnertime.

He would open his library book again and read, then drift into a daydream perhaps. Maybe the dense, musical conversations of the Late Quartets helping time along on Sundays created the framework of his constructions, but he couldn't talk about them with me.

My mother recently told me when she first met him in New York City in the 1950s he already wanted to be a writer, but he was a young man soon caught up in jobs he didn't like, finding himself in places he didn't belong. He only went to college briefly, discovering he had read all the books the professors had assigned. When I was young I understood his real work wasn't the job he went to each morning but his private occupation noting the constellations of the distant words, moving them closer, but I watched in silence, already enchanted, awaiting a peculiar fate the stories of my childhood had prepared for me.

After he left my mother I imagined him continuing his great project. For thirty years I imagined it changing, joined with my life. He moved with his new wife back to New Orleans and then San Miguel, and while he became older I began to think he was waiting for some sign before revealing something unique, the way the paths might lead to my heart, the way the world could be changed, but my doubts had been growing. Yes, in his brief letters I believed he honestly took care to remind me my simple

life was worth celebrating. Always praising the quotidian, he told me his own life was simple, in the routines of domestic pleasures, with his wife, their meals, the wine, and their animal friends, but I still saw him dreaming, studying with stubborn purpose, and building his reveries into the place of meaning. By then I was slowly losing my mind, convinced that everyone was hiding secrets from me. Everyone was a kind father, patient with my limitations, waiting for me to learn what couldn't always be expressed in words. Life looked at me so oddly, like an owl reading my thoughts.

I only visited my father twice in those thirty years, each time departing sadly, at a loss for words. Our company was not enough to inspire the kind of conversation you read about when spirits meet in chosen cities. After he died, I wondered, would a familiar song lead him through the old crowded lives of the dead, as if a book by my father could appear in their expressions? Then I found out all along he had been throwing his notes away, believing there was nothing worthwhile to save. His wife told me he had been keeping sense of practical matters, not always his contemplations. My portraits of the authors had been dissolving, the eyes I had dreamed, like islands of patience I had lost. Maybe the medical appointments and financial records were more important, the reading lists, stray thoughts and reminders. After filling one notebook, he moved to the next, discarding them like calendars.

I also learned he had thrown away my letters, one by one, after making a few notes on the envelopes to help him remember what I had written, then tossing those also after answering me in his way.

I spent so long imagining who my father was because we lived so far apart, and now I still wonder about the knowledge he took with him when he disappeared. I sit lost in my thoughts, thinking about long, complex projects, the connections between worlds, the anecdotes of pattern-keepers and mystics. I have built a small library but I've stopped riding my bicycle. I've stopped making collages. My creations already seem lost in apprehensions, in the common way time hides one in many, in obscurity.

In another dimension, and with a ghostly
energy, the Great Project comes to life, whirl-
ing with light, and memory. When was the
night we rose in joy for the Preservation Hall
Jazz Band, improvising in Royce Hall? Danc-
ing, my discovery of the sounds seemed to
begin there, a reminder of Mardi Gras and our
time in New Orleans buried inside me, and the
clarinet and cornet reaching high in my eyes for
delight. When was the first night we went to
the NuArt Theater in Los Angeles and saw the
strange smile of Alec Guinness on the screen,
catching an inkling of his humor? I remember
my father playing his harmonica and telling
strange jokes, laughing with an innocence he so
rarely showed. I remember him playing pick-
up-sticks and Blockhead at parties and open-
ing the champagne bottle. He would whistle a
tune as he rolled up in the alley on his bicycle
after work, ready to sit down on the sofa and
read. I now know often he was dreaming of
adultery.

Today I found him in some poems someone else
had written. I read them inside, the front door
open in the afternoon sunlight, listening to the

birds through the screen door. He could have written them himself. Probably he read them, more than once, years ago. I think many things I find to read will be his actual thoughts, transformed in the time it takes to listen, coming to me now to make up for our failures.

The World of the Garden

I slowly forgot about gardens for nine years in Santa Monica because my mom could only save her own garden outside near the stairs. Pots of flowers accumulated almost invisibly in a sunny alcove of the ugly apartment building, only one disheveled palm tree out front. In the little corner overlooking the alley, she continued, the resourceful colors of the hours unnoticed by me. I lost my education for watering and planting, instead becoming unsure on concrete. Skateboarding underneath in the parking garage, chasing sunlight in the doldrums, picture shows, paid for with feather pennies worn down in heavy, blue folders. For some years I thought it was enough, theoretically, to water the leaves of a plant and not the roots. Absorbing the rain this way the plant would grow. I could look down into ordinary yards below, softly within high walls of cinder blocks, finding roses only in childhood gardens, with lemon trees, poinsettias, honeysuckle vines we left behind on Chelsea Street, and even farther away, the plum tree, the dogwood, but I had become older.

I wonder how my mom built things in the alcove, saving broken plates, chipped cups, stones, the soil, pebbles, her own ceramics, practice bowls, fitting together gently the places for her flowers, because I can see so clearly her gardens to follow in Seattle, where we returned after my father left us. I looked past the alcove as I habitually walked up the stairs holding the damp, heavy laundry in my bare arms on my way to the roof. We never had a clothes dryer in Santa Monica so our clothes lasted longer, I was told.

In Seattle, in Wallingford, in an old, curious apartment building with a porch and wooden stairs, a tall hedgerow of hawthorns, my mom's allotment was the unwanted margins and odd corners all around the garden the older tenants claimed for themselves. Her herbs began to fill the cracks and crannies, in thin troughs along the garage, and borders of the alley fence, as she called up the stems and thoughts of the garden's lot with Chinese lanterns, leeks, beans, peas, tomatoes and greens. Once again she became a tinker of boxes of lettuce, her memory of arias broadcasting seeds and songs of birds feeding nests the neighbors heard on the radio through the kitchen door. Her plants made new flavors for vigorous days and explorations of pain falling from her hands.

Reading formal letters from New Orleans, spare, like archaic topiary around his Fountains of the Epicureans, and the statues of Marx, I found my father philosophizing, a drunken spirit who stood by during our visits, my mom busy cooking vegetable soup, generous wishes for almost everyone. I walked there with Rebecca, from our attic apartment in a wooden house surrounded by fruit trees, three miles away, where we slept in a small alcove with a window, our bed just fitting in.

Writing this makes me wonder about my own mind, and all the paths and crevices into the past, sometimes finding their way again to my foolish, impatient suicide attempt in that attic room when I was thirty, lying down on the bed after eating a handful of shiny laurel leaves I had picked from a hedge a few blocks away. I grow embarrassed and uneasy remembering how madness surprised me, a city untying the strings of my head to look inside, stirring a commotion of telepathy and collected hearts, filling dark rooms in an actor's soul. I was terrified, but also enchanted, revealed in this imaginary place so far from the living constructions of the world of the sturdy, vulnerable people, whose love I trusted.

After eating the leaves I didn't sleep or dream, or leave the world behind, so a few months later I bicycled to the Aurora bridge to jump off but again I was lucky. A group of workers without knowing it stopped me, so I rode on, going to the Harborview hospital. I didn't stay long that time but would return again. To escape the city I entered the heart of the city. My doctor had sent me there, without asking first, so I would have to stay for a while. Tucked away in the locked ward, with simplicity, secured and insulated in Harborview, I met the experienced story of the city's charity, as the strange and normal people changed, as we all calmed down together. The anonymous ones too became quiet, in my mind, in the city, characters no

longer diverting memory from my night twin
for the museum of the cyborgs of the future.
Even these plans became innocent again.

I regulated my days back into the present, turn-
ing a knob on the peaceful machine of the city,
suddenly domesticated like a gray cat, taking
my medicine. Rebecca, tired and very worried,
eager to free me herself, had moved our belong-
ings without me, helped by family and friends,
to an old, small house to be rented for $500 a
month, where we would recuperate for the next
two years, lucky to land in a quiet neighbor-
hood, to the south, in an out-of-the-way corner
of the city. The topsy-turvy illness collapsing the
rooms of people who are close, who are shaken
into strangers and foes, sank into the ground
like elbows and angles of rain, as we ourselves
settled in the mossy, gnarled trees, settling our
ancient, blameless debts together. Our hopeful-
ness had accidentally stored a love of safe time
in the kitchen windows, twigs of rosemary and
lavender in brown paper bags, fading thread-
bare curtains, pictures from folklore, as the
dangerous past became a familiar view of old
pear trees, and birds, apple trees and lichen.

We found a dog to live with us, Emma, to walk us around Lake Washington and Seward Park.

That was years ago, a lucky interlude in life. I still notice my imaginary world changing, breathing with me all these years, life dreaming in the hollows and clouds of the city, forming characters. I try to lengthen the time of the old alcoves the world repairs, my head like a broken cup, tipping, spilling into a book, and into a garden.

I'm sorry if I take myself too seriously, sounding lugubrious in these pages, my voice removed and distant from the past. I often wonder if the madness I first felt long ago only became a different kind of rumor, mutated by the medication which is difficult to stop taking, year after year. Or, to be charitable, am I better now than I would have been, all things considered, if I hadn't started taking the medicines, which perhaps are giving me the chance to grow old?

The Spell of the Garden

I knew I couldn't be seen but I could hear her pruning, clipping twigs, seed heads, in the silence of the old neighborhood, old because she had lived here so long, in the house beside us. I still sunbathed then, choosing a corner almost hidden from all sides, on a faded beach towel from California my father had brought back before we all flew to the hotel above the ocean. For a few strange weeks before we found a house to rent, we took the glass elevator down the side of the hotel, and I walked with my sister down the cliff stairs, forgetful, tumbling into the waves. Now I was enclosed in a small back yard on the same towel printed with a geometric tree and birds, birds like my lack of names for old schemes. School ignored them all in Santa Monica. My sister still talked to us then.

Nostalgia like electricity flickering beckons me back into my pen when I would like to be brave again in the cold salt air.

The pruning shears clicked in the shrubs and I heard leaves rustling on the other side of the green fence, then quiet, then the wind in the trees around me. I didn't know the old woman would have to move away soon. She's been away for many years now.

She found I was interested in writing and invited me over to show me a long poem she was working on in her old age, which astonished me, as the silence in the old homes became filled with her pantheistic, vibrant arguments with scholars. I had hoped for a neighbor like her all along. I began to see animals kindly thinking of me, bringing hidden forms and thoughts between people closer. It took me a long time though to recognize her hand in my mind. I wanted to believe in her poetry and allow her to worship the mythology inside it. She would calm the resentful one with difficult courage as the mystery spoke in her natural turns, the slowly changing, charming term, palimpsests.

What was it like inside her house? We sat in
the breakfast nook usually, yellow, bell-shaped
patterns on the walls, in the sunshine, or in
winter we warmed by the open oven door.
Sweets and hot chocolate, almonds, ginger
bread, and dried pears, and her chronicle of
ancient frauds, the way philosophers kept mis-
taking magicians and their books to be older
than they really were. Egypt and the sphinx,
Thrice Great Hermes, Our Lady of the Gold-
finch, in the stairwell, the sorceress was actu-
ally much more like all of us. She translated
through her hopeful curiosity, a kind lesson,
the scribe between us.

A few rainy months went by and I knew I had
to tell Rebecca, my companion, but instead
kept secrets about the old woman appear-
ing in my dreams. I leaned against a wall
in her basement, aware of being separated
from our own home, now in the distance,
but I could hear our dog barking, looking
for me. The old woman kept me in chains
but wasn't cruel, and told me she would let
me go soon.

In the kitchen we talked about poetry. Once we had an argument about Shelley's Witch of Atlas, who created a hermaphrodite to travel with through the night, flying together in a boat carved out of an enormous gourd. She knew the witch was ageless, while I had always thought of her as old. The witch flies over the sleeping city, whispering into the people's sleeping ears. When I listened to her I could catch no conscious glimmer that she knew I had been her captive. In the last dream I had about her a slow stream of sharp, tiny objects came out of my mouth, pins, nails, needles, all the things I had swallowed growing up, leaving my mouth in strange clouds, but who will sew the clothes together now, and the curtains?

Time Can Run Down

In the 1970s Altadena Dairy delivered raw milk
to our apartment in Santa Monica, obeying my
mom's wishes for her children to be healthy,
but I was born a fast runner. Our cat batted
the small bells hanging on the door above the
milk box when she wanted to come in, and I
jumped, running down the stairs to the alley, to
Lincoln Junior High, the morning after I won
the race with Raymond. I wondered if anyone
would recognize me, a few kids walking on the
other side of the street. My sweaty palm wore
away a leaf in the paper cover of the Spanish
book I carried in the morning fog. I heard a
kind of unknown mass conversing, the gossip
of a magician introducing exotic parrots to my
mother's tree. Would the inscrutable ones, sat-
isfied in their own time, be curious and talk
to me? Straggling groups of kids joined with
me, entering the schoolyard and then filling the
hallways. I imagined emanations, and echoes

of my hopeful thoughts, early confusions and breath of a monster I awoke in the alphabet, growing aware of me, looking from the scenery into my anonymous childhood.

I became wound up and couldn't concentrate in Mr. Winkhour's computer science class. Programming the computer with the command INPUT, I opened a space for another person to add their own information, a question someone could answer. The choices go inside and are considered, looping to the Random Number Generator. This generator is powerful and unpredictable especially if the range is large, the number of students in a school or the people in a city. Time can run down. Narrowing the range might have saved my heart from feeling a sadness similar to paranoia. I was a poor programmer whose simple math and logic skills earned no admiration from the boys who created complex games long before computers became popular, but I enjoyed learning the first steps, like a grammar for numbers, an algebra for stories.

Could I trace a meaning, bones, muscles, and skin for my transparent thoughts? In miniature, our ancient contest, opening the sky, tripped the machinery of my future, printing a mystery of my loneliness. I admired Raymond in a world above me, attracted by his soulful nonchalance, the kindness of his gestures. My shyness, like a mean, blind creature, dreamed on a lost planet of understanding words, dreams scribbled in fading ink, sunlight in the window of Forgotten Lessons.

In chess class Mr. Daltone taught us a new opening for pawns and knights, rooks, forming walls, avenues and old city squares for diminishing time, space around the pieces on the chessboard, each wooden figure surrounded by the others, sideways, behind, ahead. Before the race I had concentrated on the board, waiting, but my eyes watered behind my glasses. I kept dabbing my eyes. My double vision and the work to hold images together strained my eyes. Prisms aligned the left and right, above, below, and tipping my head to one side also helped. When had this started?

Without depth my body moved like an arrow into a flat world of triangles where spheres became one moment, one point enduring in an empty circle, an empty eye struggling to describe a soul, or the lasting memory of an opened mouth where the Blue Dentist filled with gold the ancestral tooth of a dog singing just inside the door of the future. Through the chess class windows on the second floor I could see the playground and the dirt track below. We would race between the curving chalk lines where you can't waver or look down, unlike in the corridors. People knew Raymond was faster than lightning, but for the race he had wrapped his knee in a bandage. I stared at it, how badly was he hurt? We lined up with the other kids. Ray wasn't a tough guy, awkward enough to be humble. He was even stronger for the long distances.

The sound of the starting gun ricocheted in the schoolyard, suddenly in a story, the old time of messengers instead of stumbling, fear balanced by steps on the earth, bringing the clock of belonging to the hills, nearby. We were running together under eucalyptus trees, up steep paths, near dry gullies and deer in Will Rogers Park two years later, training on the high school cross-country team. Everyone rested in

the shade, talking, becoming friendly in a time when our running shoes were still innocent objects, and our messages required days to carry. Raymond was becoming one of the best runners in California, and I was the mediocre competitor who wished the giant pelicans of the coast would fly down and carry me back to the Shire.

Raymond stopped running for Santa Monica High School in our senior year, even though he was the best athlete, who worked the hardest but with a sense of ease, with a beautiful, independent spirit. I didn't hold it against him, how could I? Though after all this time I still feel awkward mentioning his decision, as if I need to defend him against some kind of enemy. If I had known him better we could have talked about his reasons more, if we had been closer friends. Over the years I ponder decisions I have made without having a simple answer for anyone, dropping out of the University of Washington for example. I know he still enjoyed running, like the legendary athletes from Kenya or Ethiopia I imagined striding through the hills. We saw each other only a little at Santa Monica College, and soon after

I moved away to Seattle. I have always wished our friendship could have grown and flourished in this lonely world.

Nate Thurmond's Eyes

When I opened a package of basketball cards many years ago, I didn't know the photograph of Nate Thurmond I found inside would eventually change me, perhaps contributing to my madness. The card is a simple portrait, and there is something in his eyes that would inspire me, a candor, a mixture of the angelic with a playfulness and the pleasure of a dancer. He seemed to be looking into a world of heavenly games. Nate's position was the center and I was off to the side. As I grew up, did the picture improve my imagination, with the invisible spirit of the colorful land, San Francisco?

I stored the card in a box with the others, not looking at them as often as the years went by, almost forgetting his smile. Then, sorting through them after so much time had passed, his expression startled me. I began writing a fanciful sketch about Nate's eyes, not knowing this attempt, like a tiny seed, would grow into what I thought might be a novel, a book, about my childhood and my new life as a home-care worker. The few paragraphs grew into a ramshackle house and I almost forgot which room Nate was in, as the house became my folly. Nate's presence, his strength, disappeared inside the confusion as I rushed about, opening the doors.

I had been employed as a homecare worker for several months, helping older people, a new responsibility, when I started to write the book, when I should have waited. Describing the invisible, curious feelings wasn't easy for me. An old purpose awoke with the concerns of my duties, lists of tasks buried in the pockets of a housekeeper's dress. The ancestor served the Wine of Poverty, climbing out of the root cellar with a large hourglass, to clean off the dusty, melancholy surface in the sunlight. Memories of the old people appeared and seemed to pour through me, memories of others close to them, and memories of themselves, changing the ways I thought of myself. The visitations animated me, sometimes altering how I moved or imagined my limbs. It would happen in accidental moments, the atmosphere shifting slightly like the sand and age of the old linen closets, the way I waited, listening for the tea-kettle and an important story about rainwater.

Slowly I felt I belonged in the world, forgetting about the bitter history of reality and all my old insecurities. Someone with a calm, intuitive heart, the origin forgotten in the spectacle, might have seen me there, but was she a heretic or a Saint in disguise hoping to be trusted?

Clothes and shelter I could only partially sense held my new self who gently pushed me aside as I worked, borrowing my own heart from a dream. The equilibrium was as perishable as a glass of milk waiting near the edge of a sleepy afternoon. I seemed to be making friends with spirits but was I only performing an old role, multiplied in the reflections of my troubled mind?

Many more years have passed and I am getting old myself. My abandoned manuscript rests in a manila envelope, in a file box, but my story is still organized by madness. I often feel I am walking with another when I am alone. Someone else is stirring the food with me when I cook, and I listen to so many voices I often feel there is no need to write anymore because my thoughts are always apparent. Is this because I have close companions? After all, we are always imagining each other, filled with each other's wonder.

Not too long ago, Nate Thurmond died. He was 74 years old. Jerry West reminisced, "he played with an unbelievable intensity and was simply a man among boys on most nights, especially on the defensive end." When I was young and saw his photograph I imagined an unlikely story, but who was the real Nate Thurmond? Complicated, intelligent, and strong, maybe he will forgive me now for my childish devotion.

Nate Thurmond looked at the sky with a clear, whimsical gaze, almost startled, as he remembered he was being photographed by the card company and was inside the basketball arena.

The day after the photograph he sat down beneath the hoop's trunk to sort his collection of colorful shells from the beach, and today he had also brought rare postcards. He untied his huge shoes on the wooden floor. One of his teammates turned around to look at him as the rest of the team disappeared into the passage-way, chatting and wiping off their foreheads and necks with towels, and asked, "Nate, did you just stub your toe?"

Nate often sat by himself thinking. He looked up and smiled and waved at his friend and wiggled his toes. His teammate was reassured and joined the others for their showers. Then they all got dressed and walked through the old port city of San Francisco where the first librarian of the Oakland Free Library had once lived many years ago, the poet Ina Coolbrith. She had lost the long, detailed manuscript she had been writing about the history of literature in California when her apartment was ruined in the fire of 1906. Her comforting homes had been places where her friends gathered to talk and often to listen to her sing and play her guitar she'd learned in the Spanish-American style when she was a child growing up in the small pueblo Los Angeles where her family had moved in 1855.

Isadora Duncan wrote, "There was a public library in Oakland where we then lived, but no matter how many miles we were from it, I ran or danced or skipped there and back. The librarian was a very wonderful and beautiful woman, a poetess of California, Ina Coolbrith. She encouraged my reading, and I thought she always looked pleased when I asked for fine books. She had very beautiful eyes that glowed with burning fire and passion.*

Nate Thurmond's eyes were wonderful for the center, who has to see all around as the other players circle his pivot, the anchor that has to be able to fly also, carrying the four people in a fast movement he or she balances with bending knees, and soaring hands and arms. The large wings of the invisible bird floated back and forth within the periphery of his eyes.

* My information about Ina Coolbrith comes from the marvelous book Ina Coolbrith, Librarian and Laureate of California, by Josephine DeWitt Rhodehamel and Raymond Wood.

Science Fiction and Lunacy

The old downtown Seattle Public Library was almost removed in reality (the building cannot be photographed) yet afternoons in the old library remain inside the city. Many admire the new library, I know, and delight in the towering glass walls, finding it important and amazing, the mazes of aisles in the center, deep inside the zigzagging glass, and seeing the sky divided everywhere around them. I don't deny circulation has gone up, and there is more room for new books and computers.

Computers of different sizes, shapes, and colors are like mirrors people look through, toward the other side, feeling along a line to the world, photographs, playing, colorful, exact, emotional, difficult jobs in the expensive city. I don't picture computers as harmful machines, but sometimes I wonder where imagination has gone, trying to perfect digital technology.

Ecology and harmony are goals of both angels and reasonable people, like William Blake's Sweet Science, but community, belonging, sadness and joy will always be complex, with no perfect solution waiting in the future. Impossible afternoons in a garden glimpsed through a keyhole, the beginning of a dream is often hidden in the past, with lessons.

I lost my way in the new library and couldn't find the wooden sculpture of Alice, or James Washington's beautiful stone bird-animal. The new library is disorienting, but the city grows accustomed to the future, with the children. Science fiction distorts my memories, and my perspective on the present. I remember the light of the old library, the world of thoughts, a domestic light inside the world. Are the new branch libraries becoming our memory theaters in the neighborhoods? Tended plants, walls of vines, and trees surround them. Will funds last into the future for the city gardens, books and gardens?

A few letters regret the passage of the old library, describing simpler escalators passing each other in the tall central chamber, walls of small lemon-colored tiles (old mosaics fill the volume, another land) or taking the elevator to the Art and Music room on the 4th floor. People remember the rooms clearly or faintly, the details bright then fading, as they remember books and records, elevator doors opening, tables they sat at to read. Most of these books are still somewhere in the new library, in the same order, more or less, shouldn't that reassure us? The contents of my old character are still inside, but don't forget, there was another library, even older, a third library. Sometimes I think of resting inside the old library, here at home, where we are almost hidden by hedges, inside the multiplying, small bowers of leaves and sunshine. I save my common memory of my parents bringing me to the Last Exit on Brooklyn in the late 1960s, where chessboards were stored under the long wooden tables, where I drank hot apple cider in that room with the high windows, now humming with mathematical tutoring.

I didn't ask a librarian where the sculptures are now, but I'm sure one could have told me. What do the old librarians think, the old library in their minds as they work, remembering the sections, the geometry of rectangles, flowering pages, their old desks, the shelved dolphin-feelings, porpoise stamps of the old library, the phantom library's vital questions? It is dangerous to think too hard about the whole block being torn down and replaced, then the memories are filled with dust, and moving around suffocates us, so build the contemplation of happiness where you can.

In my memories glass display cases exhibit odd, antique musical instruments at the foot of the escalators and upstairs in the Art and Music room rests the heavy book reproducing colorful Diamond Star baseball cards from the Depression. The rare volume of Leonora Carrington's paintings, published in Mexico. The Aldo Ciccolini records of Satie. All these seeds now multiply years later in my own September library needing shelves near Apollinaire's archetypal lemon trees, Poetry on the ground floor, whimsical sections discovering type forming calligrammes. St. Bea's Bread growing in the future of John Crowley's *Engine Summer*. Janet Frame's shy volumes of autobiography, child and mother of the books that saved her life, as she escaped the asylum. The archaic lyrics of "Flowers of the Forest." We all have our own catalog, our own shelves inside our senses, the ears and eyes of friends, librarians, generations and chance.

So, I have decided. I will make my headquarters here. We will visit each other, writing the call numbers on slips of paper with short pencils for spirits reading every version of our natures. I will return to the circles and squares remaining, curved fountains, rectangular moments with luck and limits. The science fiction plot may unfold now, and the mystery, and we won't be afraid, even though the world is ending. I will travel to the old library, on various bus lines, like a vagabond because our house needs to repair our hearts and the happenstance of the future, the eventualities of aging. Concerns for each other sound in my mind like the whole city talking through dreams, through the air, into structures of time, where people gather our minds together. Yet telepathy becomes a selfish, unreliable belief, I know, and when I talk on the telephone with my mom who is so old now, when I hear her actual voice, and when I visit her, I feel grateful for many reasons. Doctors and nurses help her now, along with friends and family, asking Computers of Long Life for better record-keeping and communication. Bringing medicines and kind activities, companions recognize her strong spirit, in the Land of Hope where often I feel neglectful and cowardly, hiding in my old way.

You look out the windows toward the distant Olympic mountain range and Puget Sound. You might take the elevator up to the little library on the 5th floor of the old building, where it is usually quiet and peaceful, maybe falling asleep with a book in your hands. You remember it's time to go down to eat at your table with your friends. Still delighted, hoping for sunshine, though you are losing your sight, hearing, and memory, you think ahead to your next Art Class, and to Exercise Class, or to helping one of the children read, even the difficult boy whose mind is hard to understand. He is both bashful and proud, wary and perhaps secretive, like your son. He takes a lot of energy to teach. In the Norse Home Retirement Community garden your friends put up a raised bed for salad greens, by the fountain, and the baseball games are beginning at last.

The suspense of a book I don't want to finish reading leads me forward, accompanied by unsettling emotions, the shocked feelings of someone who never had to grow up until now. I have to keep reading. I want to understand the scale of purple blocks and spires of music in the city, in the far reaches of time, voices welling up inside me, notes, and tears. Did I really create a Radio of Worry, adapting to the strange currents of sand in the water, the paranoia of my brain?

My pearl, the bright, fictitious transistor in my head, where the voices turn around and around, chasing their words like fishes in the sea, only guesses you can hear me, when my privacy and silence are lost. So I play a small role on the radio, damaged and half-empty, talking after others place the missing spring and filament in the song, in the hours loaned to me by women. What can I offer? Eventually, I grow so sad when I talk with all of you. My subconscious, wooden and glass face blurs into the outside world, the letters of old-fashioned ancient atoms becoming pictures on those strange Pythagorean stations, on the frequency of luck. Who turns the little dial of my fate in dreams?

I am responsible. The characters change, groups gathering, dispersing, pleased or disappointed with me, responding in that land like flocks of birds in the sky, or packs of dogs in a field near the dragonflies. Can I make peace with you? The structure of a safe home in my mind cannot withstand totality, and the circling seasons are weighing us down. The rats in the crawl-space are gone, the holes carefully blocked with sturdy wire, the little, low door strengthened, but when I turn to look the creatures are still nesting in our ears at night. I'm afraid of the towering fir trees falling down from across the street onto our house in a storm. Even in summer I remember how they sway, how the rain takes up our eyes, the rain we love. The crack in the foundation from the earthquake is almost covered behind the many lives of the blue globe thistles, almost hidden, in the summer, and I'm still afraid of the pond next door overflowing and seeping.

Going outside, I wonder who arranges the small dramas, as if they were meant to startle us, to help us learn about ourselves, on the buses, in the shops, in the parks, where the homeless people sleep. In London, long ago, the Metropolitan

Lunacy Commission truncated the poor souls of the mad, but can we discover here the kind, marvelous ways the imagination works? Some problems are hard to solve and I live a sheltered life. Sometimes it seems all I have for a job is thinking and walking. The worn earth paths through the ruins of the naval base, now Magnuson Park, by the lake, wind through fields of grass as tall as our knees, our waists, our shoulders, our heads, as our old dog, Emma, leads us along.

When I travel to Wallingford I visit the long, narrow waiting room of the Community Psychiatric Clinic on Stone Way, the reception station with the sliding-glass windows, and the inner offices, the pharmacy, all located where people once bought and sold old clothes, books, and kitchen utensils, odds and ends, in the second-hand store operated by the patients of the clinic. Once, I browsed through the clothes before my appointments. I remember a pair of dark green cotton pants I bought and wore for many years until they became tattered, one of many pairs I purchased, after deliberating in the dressing room, glimpsing my new face in the mirror. When I sit in the waiting room

I remember the cluttered but tidy, calm area, and all the brave, courteous case managers, nurses, and doctors from my past and present, who offered help wisely, as they stepped out of the mystery into a familiar city where I belong with the others.

Would you like to rest a little longer, they ask? Maybe it's time to get to work? You need strength to bear the sensibility of your voices, the convincing nonsense, thoughts in disguises acting in your head, ghosts and souls of the living avenues travelling to a stage in your body. We need funding in the city, and space, housing for the hard times ahead.

The seemingly autonomous City Parks and Recreation Department mailed out obscure maps of the old fields, erasing for the future some of the wild areas, for sports fields, but also for brand new paths, new wetlands. Sometimes in the waiting room I see the paths in the grass, the stands of poplars, hawthorns, and birches. Meandering through the shade and growth of nooks and crannies, in dappled sunlight under the leaves, birds flying, the small world of blue distances guided our eyes and footsteps through each moment worn on the paths. I remember discovering part of a path one morning, not knowing where it would go, trees filling the horizon beyond the grasses we entered. Emerging slowly through a thicket we walked along by the top of an old cement wall, the path following the lip of stone, but hidden from below, sloping down until we reached the familiar paved walkway we had taken many times to the lake. How strange to feel lost in the city park.

Sometimes when I sit here I remember an inside wall of my mother's old apartment, a few blocks from the clinic, on Woodland Park Avenue, a wall between her dining room and her neighbors, a wall with two doors opening into two long closets under the slanting ceiling of a stairwell leading to the next floor, through the middle of the old building. Beautifully printed wallpaper, torn slightly, layered and worn, lined the doubled alcoves one could walk into, filled with clothes and trunks that had travelled and circled back from Japan, Baltimore, New Orleans, and Santa Monica. Memory holds me in the old building where many of the neighbors were our friends. An architecture of sentiment inside located before us a sense of curiosity, a feeling of kindness in this flimsy, teetering city barely held up by work and effort, intricate equations, training lengths and wheels, carrying. I knew the people on the other side were curious also, in our school of personality, but I did deserve a lesson. *The Wonder Clock*, by Howard Pyle, contained many portals in the stories for childhood, as the youngest one who was lazy, an honest simpleton, warming his toes by the ashes, at last wanders off, looking for fortune, with the older clever ones, the ones I became more and more like, I'm afraid.

What can I find here, opening my wooden and cardboard file-boxes, opening my homes from the past for a history of peculiar families making notes to populate shadows, on the margins, in a world of childhood radios? We picture the voices deep inside the clouds, the sky, the voices of the moon tuning the electricity of invention for the sun to keep shining. Kept in the dark, this mistaken meditation on the city has haunted me for a long time, as the connections grow into alarming thickets, sharp thorns and decisions out in the world.

I will always worry about shelter and safekeeping. Many new ways of storing memories are being invented but we are still forgetful. Maybe I am waiting to read the books some of you will write about Seattle, because I am hopeful, too. Another dog, our beloved Nyssa, began living with us nine years ago, while I was waiting, when these pages were stored away. She walked with Emma's ghost on the paths I mention, and played with us in our backyard, but she too is gone now. We will always remember her with great fondness and joy. I started working again on these pages during the last month of her life. Today the hummingbird visited the spring flowers, and a little beetle hurried across the bricks, both wishing Nyssa Happy Birthday.

I think of resting inside the old library, here at home, where we are almost hidden by the hedges, inside the multiplying small bowers of leaves and sunshine.

CARLO LEVY has lived in seven different neighborhoods of Seattle, where he was born in 1961. He is the author of a book of poems entitled *The Radio Factory* (also with original collages). In 1998 he received the first annual Nelson Bentley Award given by the editors at *Fine Madness*, for his poem, "The Old Music of Heraclitus." He is married to Rebecca Alexander, a painter, poet, librarian, and gardener.

www.ingramcontent.com/pod-product-compliance
Lightning Source LLC
Chambersburg PA
CBHW051644120626
46551CB00015B/2213